HOW TO WRITE A NOVEL THE EASY WAY USING THE PULP FICTION METHOD

JIM DRIVER

Join the Writers' VIP Club

MEMBERS OF JIM DRIVER'S *WRITERS' VIP Club* get free books, articles and videos about writing and self-publishing. They are always the first to hear about new books and events.

See the back of this book for details on how you can sign up for free.

First Things First

I WILL SHOW you how to write a novel using my *Pulp Fiction* Method. It's a system I developed to help me write quality novels as quickly as possible.

Like the pulp writers of the Golden Age (roughly 1910-1960), the modern author must write quickly and without distraction.

Since the first version of this book appeared in 2014, the way I work has changed over time. Later editions reflect those improvements and include a mountain of new material, including several new chapters.

I'm a big fan of Pulp Fiction. Not just the Tarantino movie but all those great magazine stories and paperback novels that appeared in the first half of the 20th century. Raymond Chandler, Dashiel Hammett, Louis L'Amour, Isaac Asimov, John D MacDonald, Jim Thompson, James M Cain, F Scott Fitzgerald, Edgar Wallace, and many others all got their start writing cheap fiction to order.

Pulp novels were often cleverly plotted and sometimes remarkably well-written. Quite a few were adapted into great movies, including *The Killer Inside Me*, *The Grifters*, *The Postman Always Rings Twice*, and *Mildred Pierce*. They weren't all masterpieces by any means, but thousands were written, and millions of readers enjoyed them.

Authors of pulp novels were paid by the word. They had to produce great stories in as short a time as possible. They didn't have word processors or computers to help them, every word had to be hand-written or battered out on a manual typewriter.

If they made a mistake, they had to rip out the paper and start the whole page again. As a result, pulp writers learned techniques that allowed them to write fast and furiously without making costly mistakes. They didn't have time for writer's block or self-doubt. If they didn't write, they didn't eat.

I'm going to show you methods that work. My advice will enable you to write your novel quickly and easily.

This is a short book: only around 20,000 words. I'm assuming that you need useful information, not waffle. To be a writer, you've got to knock out the words, not sit around reading books about how to do it.

I'm not going to try and

reinvent the wheel and tell you exactly how to tackle every stage of the writing process. I'm going to give you the basics, plus lots of valuable tips, and tell you where to find out more, should you need it.

If you were looking for a great big *how-to-do-everything* kind of book, stop reading now and get a refund. If you genuinely want to write a novel and start selling on digital platforms like iBooks and Kindle for Amazon, carry on reading…

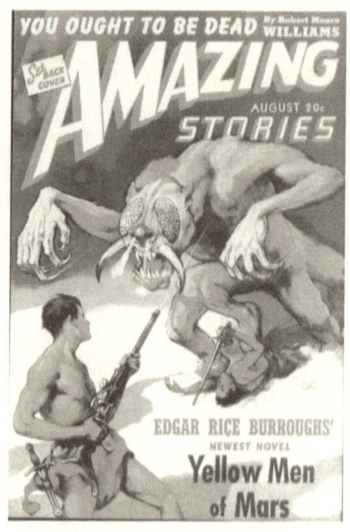

You Are Already A Writer

Have you ever written an email or a school essay? Assuming you have, you are already a writer. Going on to write a novel is simply a matter of scaling up.

Writing novels is really not as difficult as you think. I've written several myself, though none (so far) under my own name — it's a long story. I've ghostwritten seven novels, and the other sixteen (so far) have been published under pseudonyms.

You can definitely write a novel. All you need is someone to tell you how to do it as simply as possible. That's where I come in. But first, it's time for some home truths.

You Are A Terrible Writer

You may be a writer, but the bad news is that you are almost certainly a dreadful writer. The good news is practically everyone is, at least, to start with.

Do you suppose the first time the great English cabinet maker Thomas Chippendale (1718-1779) picked up a chunk of wood, he was able to create an intricately inlaid cabinet like the one above?  Not a chance. Just like everyone else, he began as a raw amateur, and he practised until he got better.

Chippendale could have wasted years reading books on making cabinets and bemoaning the fact that he wasn't as good as he thought he needed to be. Luckily, he didn't. He learned the basic skills and threw himself into the task. In the end, all his efforts paid off.

What is it about writing that makes new authors despair when they can't write a literary masterpiece at their first attempt? No other job has similar expectations. You don't become a plumber and think you'll be able to fit a central heating system your first morning on the job. Would-be pianists aren't shocked when they can't play Beethoven's *Sonata Hammerklavier opus 106* the first time they sit down at a piano.

So, get real!

The first hurdle is to accept that your writing probably isn't brilliant. Believe me, no one (except you) expects it to be.

Just get over yourself!

Most magazines and books produced today aren't that well written, yet the people who write them still get paid.

It doesn't mean you can't make a living writing just because you're not a devastatingly good writer. Thousands of bad authors make plenty of money. In fact, being good doesn't guarantee you a pay rise. Often the reverse is true.

It may surprise you that people don't always want

the best. Otherwise, we'd all be getting our clothes hand-made by master tailors; the most watched television programs would be clever BBC documentaries and art-house films instead of *American Idol, Love Island,* and *Australia's Fattest Loser.*

Only a tiny percentage of people insist on buying the best. The rest of us are quite happy getting stuff off the peg and from the bargain bin. It's the same with books. *Literary Fiction* is one of the lowest-selling categories online. Most people want cheap schlock with a fairly decent story — books about vampires, zombies, murder mysteries, erotic encounters, and so on.

Think you can manage cheap schlock with a fairly decent story?

You bet you can!

That's what I'm going to show you in this short book. Your writing will improve as you go on, but never beat yourself up. You can write a sellable novel right now. You just need to be told the nuts and bolts of how to do it.

The second hurdle to cross is closely linked to the first. It's what I call…

The Curse Of The Writer

It took me a long time to work this out, but the *Curse of the Writer* is that people who are drawn to writing have a better-than-average sense of criticism. Simply put, they can tell good writing from bad.

If you're not a creative person, this is a great skill to have (especially if you're a reviewer), but for writers, it generally leads to trouble.

When an author looks over a chapter that's just been written, it's easy to think, *this is awful.* I still do it myself. Inside my head, my subconscious is comparing it to other stuff I've read. Maybe to writing by really great authors. I appreciate I'm not as good as they are, so what I've written must be not only terrible but also *totally unacceptable.*

This voice in the head is the #1 cause of writers giving up. Writers who don't give up and get published either don't realise they are terrible or don't care. You have to be like them. Ignore what your brain tells you, and you're well on your way to becoming a successful writer.

This is how you can do it:

Forget about being a critic. You are a worker, and your product is words and sentences on a page. When you read something you've written, ask yourself these three questions:

1. Does it make sense?
2. Is what I am trying to say clear and to the point?
3. Does it advance the story in some way?

If the answer to every one of these questions is *yes*, then what you've written is good enough. If not, you just need to edit. I'll show you how to do that later.

Simple Is Good

If you were going to follow in William Chippendale's footsteps and take up carpentry, you'd start with something simple, like a letter rack or a small toy truck, right? You'd be an idiot to attempt an intricately carved, bow-fronted rosewood cabinet as your first project.

It's even more true with a novel. Simple is good and many of our best writers, such as Elmore Leonard, Raymond Chandler and Ernest Hemingway, kept it simple their entire lives.

As I said, I'm a big fan of

Pulp Fiction: it's easy to read and contains great storylines. Just take a look at this randomly-selected extract from *The Fabulous Clipjoint* by Fredric Brown to give you an idea of what I mean:

The coffee was cold and Mom started to get some fresh, but Uncle Ambrose said, "Let's go down and have a drink instead. What say, Bassett?"

The detective shrugged. "Okay by me. I'm off duty now."

Mom shook her head. "You two go," she told them.

I dealt myself in, said I was thirsty and wanted some Seven–Up or a coke. Uncle Ambrose said, "Sure," and Mom didn't squawk, so I went downstairs with them.

We went to a place on Grand Avenue. Bassett said it was a quiet place where we could talk. It was quiet all right; we were almost the only ones in there.

We took a booth and ordered two beers and a Coca–Cola. Bassett said he had to phone somebody and went back to the phone booth.

I said, "He's a nice guy. I kind of like him."

My uncle nodded slowly. He said, "He's not dumb

and he's not honest and he's not a louse. He's just what the doctor ordered."

"Huh? How do you know he's not honest?" I wasn't being naive; I know plenty of coppers aren't; I just wondered how Uncle Ambrose could be so sure so quick—or if he was just talking through his hat.

"Just looking at him," he said. "I don't know how, but I know. I used to run a mitt−camp with the carney, Ed. It's a racket, sure, but you get so you can size people up."

For me, this kind of writing ticks all the boxes. It is:

- Easy to understand.
- Natural and easy to read. You don't have to go back and reread anything to find out what the author meant.
- Imparts information and moves the story along.

Pulp writers were badly paid, and their novels – usually Mystery, Science Fiction, Fantasy, Horror, Detective, War, and Westerns – were sold cheaply. To make a living, they had to write quickly and often. They couldn't risk falling out with the publishers by padding their books with extra words. Their job was to tell stories in a way everyone, even the badly educated, could understand. Many great authors learned their craft this way.

I was editor-in-chief at a small publishing house for ten years. I am now going to reveal to you the main reason publishers reject most novels by first-time authors: it's because almost all of them feel the need to over-write.

Instead of writing *the cat sat on the mat*, an eager young writer might come up with something like: "The proud little tabby cat had fur that glistened in the soft afternoon sunlight that was peculiar to the section of New Hampshire in which his matriarch resided. An observer who squinted his or her eyes in a certain manner and looked particularly closely could discern muted browns, darker mocha, Brazilian coffee, olive greeny-browns and so many more strident colours." And so it goes on, and on, and the cat's not even seen the mat yet.

This kind of flabby writing isn't good and will certainly not hold any reader's attention for long. An essential part of a good novel is that it engages the reader and keeps them engaged from the first sentence right to the very last word.

In many ways, self-publishing (Kindle and the like) is the modern equivalent of the Pulps. The big difference is that now everyone has an equal opportunity to become a paid writer.

Thanks to digital outlets like iBooks and Amazon, modern writers like us don't need to go through the laborious processes of finding an agent or persuading a publisher that our work is good enough. It's now possible to publish your own novel in just a few minutes. The pay's better, too.

Instead of less than 10% royalty rates, Amazon pays between 35% and 70%. This helps explain why there's a new breed of successful authors quickly writing novels, non-fiction, and short stories to sell on Amazon and other platforms.

Are you ready to join them?

TWO

Preparing To Write

What To Write

YOU MIGHT ALREADY KNOW what kind of novel you want to write. If so, great. If not, let me suggest a way to find out. If you're hoping to make a living from your work, you've got to admit that writing novels other people will want to read makes perfect sense. The best way to do this is by seeing exactly what's selling right now.

Go to Amazon.com:

https://www.amazon.com/Best-Sellers-Kindle-Store-eBooks/zgbs/digital-text/

This should bring up a page that looks like this (obviously, the titles will be different):

Make sure the *Top 100 Paid* tab at the top-left is live (underlined in orange); we're not really interested in what's being downloaded for free. These listings include Non-fiction titles, but by clicking on the categories in the column on the left-hand side, you'll be able to hone in on the genres that interest you.

Take a good look. Go deeper by clicking the category links. Under *Mystery, Thriller & Suspense*, for example, you'll find other sub-categories. Click on a book's title to take an even closer look. By looking at the *Product Details* of an individual eBook, you'll be able to find more specific sub-categories like this:

Use the *Back* button of your browser to retrace your steps.

I suggest you concentrate on the Amazon.com site because this is the world's biggest market for self-published authors. Even if you're based outside the USA, as I am, you'll almost certainly get most of your revenue from there. In my case, and I just checked, sales in the United States account for 66.4% of my income. Next is the UK (at a paltry 19.1%), with the rest of the world making up the remaining 14.5%.

In case you're wondering, no one aside from Amazon and the author in question knows exactly how many copies of these ebooks are being downloaded. Sales relating to a ranking vary from day to day and from month to month. I've heard that a number one bestseller at Christmas might sell more than twice as many copies as the #1 in April or May.

Even so, it's safe to say that the #1 paid ebook in Kindle Store will be shifting at least 3,500 copies daily, maybe 5,000 or more. Even the #500 title should be selling 100-300 every day. And that's just taking into account sales in the USA. Plenty of other lucrative Amazon websites serving the UK, Canada, Australia, Europe, and beyond will sell these books. If you get it right, it's possible to earn massive amounts of money writing pulps for sale online.

Most Kindle authors do pretty well by regularly writing and publishing new books. In simple terms, the more they write, the more they earn. I know plenty of writers who hardly ever trouble the bestseller lists but who consistently make $300-$500 a month from each of their novels. When you've published a dozen or more, it adds up to big money.

Don't forget Amazon is just the tip of the iceberg. Other digital retailers, like iBooks and Smashwords, sell tons of books, too. Amazon tries to get you to give them the exclusive when you sign up to KDP Select, but sometimes it's best to play the field. Once you get started, the choice is entirely yours.

The big secret is to write, write, write.

Of course, first of all, you need to know what kind of books you should be writing.

Write What You Know?

The usual advice given to beginners is that they should *write what you know*. That was a good tip in the days before the Internet, Google Street View, and Wikipedia. Now it's easy to research places, dates, and people, so this advice rarely applies.

My version of the adage is that you should *write what you read*. If you enjoy reading Gothic Horror novels or watching shows like that on TV, that's what you should be writing. It'll be more enjoyable for you, plus you'll be more likely to be aware of conventions specific to the genre.

For instance, your Detective novel wouldn't be very popular with Mystery aficionados if the killer turned out to be someone who'd not previously appeared in the story or who vanishes from the scene of the crime in a Time Machine.

Similarly, I'm told readers of classic Boy-Meets-Girl

Romances wouldn't appreciate a violent fight scene in chapter three or a graphic sex romp in chapter seven.

Your success depends on getting good online reviews and through building up a 'fan base' of readers who enjoy your work enough to want to read more than one of your books. This means you have to give them what they want and what they expect and keep doing it. Usually, this entails nothing more than staying true to the conventions.

When I research what I'm going to write, I look for novels I'd like to read that are already selling well. Then I put on my surgeon's gloves to perform a series of autopsies.

Books in the Kindle bestseller charts are of two main types. Some are digital versions of print titles published by mainstream publishing houses; others are self-published by individual authors like you and me. You can almost always tell them apart by inspecting the *Product Details* on the book's Amazon page.

I usually prefer to analyse self-published titles (and not those published by mainstream publishers) because sales of these novels will not be influenced by potentially massive publicity budgets or affected by how well the print version is selling.

I buy and read as many bestsellers as I can afford, making notes as I go along. These are the kind of things I want to know:

- Who is the lead character (What is he or she like? Job? Mannerisms? etc.)
- What is the lead character's goal?

- Who or what is trying to stop the lead character from achieving their goal?
- *How is the story told (viewpoint)? First-person? Second person? From an overview?*
- How many chapters are there?
- How long are the chapters?
- How long is the finished novel?

Most of these details can be found by checking out Amazon's *Look Inside* feature. A reasonably good source of similar books can be found under the *Products related to this item* heading:

You might have to scroll past the first few 'sponsored items' (i.e. paid advertising by publishers) to see what you want. Amazon used to have a much more useful (for us, anyway) feature called 'Customers who bought this item also bought', but that seems to have been done away with in the interests of selling advertising.

Although not ideal, these 'Products related' items will give you an idea of more books in your potential market. Sometimes they'll all be by the same author. I look closely at 5-10 books that are selling well in a particular genre and pay special attention to the number of chapters and their length. Very often, readers in some genres prefer long chapters; in others, they like them shorter.

I always check out Amazon reviews for novels that interest me, paying special attention to the 1- to 3-star ones. These tell you what people think is wrong with these books. Often you can pick up a tip or two. Remember not to take reviews too seriously (especially about your own books) because there is a high proportion of nuts out there with nothing better to do than to slate other people's hard work.

When you've finished researching, you'll have a great idea of what's popular in your chosen genre and how the most successful novels have been structured in terms of length and chapters. There will invariably be maverick titles, but generally speaking, you'll be surprised at how many will follow the same pattern.

As the old showbiz saying goes: *Give people what they want, and they'll come back for more.* By following the example of bestselling titles in your genre, you'll be making your own novel much more likely to succeed.

Note: Although this book is primarily aimed at writers who want to self-publish online, most of what I say also applies to anyone who yearns to be picked up by a traditional publisher. Mainstream publishers and literary agents are perpetually looking for the next big seller, which means they could be even more influenced by commercial factors than indie authors.

The Germ Of A Story

Now you've found a genre you'd be happy to write; it's time to get down to the details.

Whatever you do, do *not* copy anyone else's ideas. Aside from being immoral and illegal, it's also bad for business and unnecessary. You'll be surprised how easy it is to be original.

I suggest you create a main character (or characters) about which you can write a series of novels. This will save you from having to keep coming up with new characters and situations all the time. Plus, it'll help you sell more books.

A similar option is to write a *saga*: a series of books that follows a family through the generations or tracks the progress of an item (such as a book or a painting) through various stages of its history.

Books linked like this can be cross-promoted and always sell more than standalone titles. As every shop-keeper knows, it's better to sell multiple items to one customer than to find multiple customers to sell a single item to. Sell multiple items to multiple customers, and you're really in business!

To start with, you'll need to decide on:

- *Period (contemporary or some time in the past or future)*
- *Place (primary locations where the story takes place)*
- *Lead Character(s)*

I'll give two examples of how I might do this, writing in two different genres.

1. Romance

The *Romance* genre covers a multitude of sins, from innocent boy meets girl stories to much more steamy fare. *Erotic Romance* is a coded way of saying 'Erotica for women'. I suggest men steer clear of this type of fiction, especially the stronger stuff. Women expect a different approach that few men, especially beginners, can satisfy.

One genre I picked up on is *Inspirational Romance*. This is particularly big in the USA, the world's most lucrative ebook market. On the day I looked, all of the top 10 in the genre's bestseller list were in Kindle's Top 1,000 of paid sales, which means they are all selling anything between 100-3,500 copies a day. Not bad, eh?

The special Romance website PublicBookshelf.com says of *Inspirational Romance*:

> A romantic relationship can be intertwined with spiritual or religious beliefs. The characters in an inspirational romance novel often find themselves dealing with the challenges of their feelings, needs and desires within the tapestry of their beliefs and the beliefs of those around them.
>
> These faith-based, inspirational Romance novels can be set in historical or contemporary settings with the themes of decency, fidelity, honesty and forgiveness.

My eye was drawn to the #10 book in this genre, which is by a veteran Canadian author, Janette Oke. She has written over seventy books, many of them series-based. I know I said it's best to look at books by authors who publish themselves rather than those signed to mainstream publishers, but Janette Oke offers a great example within a genre few writers would ever consider. *I'm the teacher and can break the rules if I choose!*

An Amazon review of *Love Comes Softly #1*, billed as "The Original Christian Fiction Series! Book one", sums up the story very well:

> Marty is a young pioneer woman, recently widowed and pregnant with no place to live and no means to go home. Clark Davis asks her to be his wife of "convenience" since he needs a caretaker for his young daughter, Missie, and Marty needs food and shelter. Not at all interested, but desperately in need, she accepts. This first book explains the first 6-8 months of this strange marriage. Marty is determined to pull her weight and do her time until Spring when Clark has agreed to pay her way home. The book is wholesome, funny, suspense filled and holds the reader's interest from cover to cover.

My author's take on it is that Janette Oke writes simply but well. The story is uncomplicated but cleverly written and makes you want to find out what happens next. Being an agnostic male, I'm way outside the book's target audience, but I happily read it to the end. One of the 2-star Amazon reviews contained a telling line: "I felt the reading level to be more appropriate for my 13-year-old niece." To me, that's a major reason this series has sold in its millions: everyone and anyone can understand it.

Love Comes Softly contains cleverly-crafted central characters and combines *Little House On the Prairie*-type cosiness with a tale of two people growing closer in the face of mutual adversity. There's also a cute step-daughter, which helps. Bad things happen to them, but the family survive and gradually Marty comes to embrace the Christian faith of her new husband.

If we were going to write an Inspirational Romance series, we'd need to find an original situation that would appeal to Janette Oke's readers. To follow the lead of *Love Comes Softly*, you'd need to create an unlikely couple (male and female) and throw them together against extreme opposition. In the original series, the opposition comes mainly from Nature and the harsh Western environment.

Where and when are we going to set our story? I thought about it for a few minutes and came up with these options: the gold fields of the Australian 1850s; the Klondike in the 1890s (more Gold Rush!); farmers in 19th century Africa; Roman Christians trying to make a life for themselves in bandit-torn early Britain; and, a family in north-east England around the 9th Century subjected to Viking raids. I'm sure you can think of even better situations.

Because it's basically a Romance, we are going to need two main characters. It's simpler to make them man and wife and, following Ms Oke's lead, we could have them brought together in less than ideal circumstances. Perhaps a slave married to his or her rescuer? Or some kind of arranged marriage? There are lots of possibilities.

If I was going to write this series, I'd start with Harold, a 20-year old Saxon nobleman who was enslaved by the Vikings when he was six. He escapes on a raid to Northumbria and hides out in caves until the Vikings give up plundering and return by sea to their own lands.

Matilda is nearly thirty-five, and has three children aged between five and twelve. Her husband has been killed by the Vikings and she is about to lose the family farm unless she can marry someone able and willing to work it. Maybe she spent the early part of her life as a nun?

Although Harold plans to return to his family home in Wessex, he and Matilda meet up, and after a big row, they realise they could be useful to one another. So, they get together. The villagers don't like it, especially the bad guy (Ethelred?), who is trying to buy the farm and marry Matilda.

For convention's sake (maybe we could create a stroppy village priest?), Harry and Matty are forced to marry. The story is driven by conflict: her being his social superior (despite his noble birth, which is pretty academic as he's so far from home); the difference in their ages; the opposition of her children and the hostility of the villagers (especially Ethelred); the danger of the Viking raiders; and so on…

You can see how easy it is the take the elements of a

successful book series and use it to fashion another that's totally different and highly original. I think it would be similar enough to attract the same readers. Because the story is so strong, it could be possible to remove the Christian element altogether.

I don't suggest you write an Inspirational Romance yourself — I certainly can't see myself doing it — but I use the example to show how the process can work, even in a genre where expectations are as tightly-restricted as this.

2. Detective Story

Murder always sells. Let's say you decide to write a Murder Mystery. Most of the books I found when I researched had a British police detective as the lead. OK, let's see what we can do with this. Of course, you can set your story anywhere in the world you choose.

The best-known modern British detectives are probably Ian Rankin's Rebus, a bitter Scotsman near retirement in Edinburgh; Mark Billingham's Tom Thorne, who is younger but still bitter and based in North London; and Peter Robinson's DCI Banks, who is quite arty and who lives in a fictional North Yorkshire town.

Step 2 involves mixing up the lead detective's characteristics.

The obvious way to go is to make your detective a woman: you don't have to; it's just one option. Pick a location: I decided London is pretty well saturated with literary cops, Oxford has Morse, and Nottingham has John Harvey's Polish-British sandwich-eating DCI

Charlie Resnick, amongst others. So, I'd go to Google maps and look for another location.

I'll go for a female police detective who's quite insecure but loves collecting vintage cars, which most women aren't known for. I like that. Because of no better reason than I was visiting the seaside yesterday, she can live and work on the South Coast of England (Brighton? Hastings? Bournemouth?). Peter James and one or two others have made Brighton their own, so maybe look at Hastings?

Let's also say our lead character can never hold down a relationship. It's probably been done, but I've personally never read anything like this, so I'd be prepared to go with it.

It's a tried-and-test rule that most detectives have a *foil*. Someone, like Sherlock Holmes' Dr Watson, they can explain things to and who they can 'riff off'. Most of the famous sidekicks have backgrounds and characteristics that are the opposite of those of the lead. For my female detective, how about an embittered older man who is close to retirement, secretly gay, but who won't admit it? It sounds to me like that might work.

Incidentally, those character traits came straight off the top of my head as I was writing this. It's amazing how easily things slot into place when you get your brain working. The great thing is that everything can be altered, improved, and changed in the *Outlining* process.

Generating The Story Idea

By now, you should have an idea of the book you will be writing. You might even have the situation and the main characters already worked out. If not, don't worry: it'll come.

In another of my books, *How To Write A Million Dollar Story*, I show you eight ways to pluck story ideas out of the air. Here are three of them:

1. What If?

You've already sorted your genre, or at least narrowed it down to one or two you like the look of. Each of them will have its own particular possibilities. For example, in Detective Fiction, there's invariably a murder. This might lead you to ask, *What if the President of the United States murdered someone?* Or, *What if a pathologist murdered someone and then messed with the evidence during an autopsy?*

Think of unlikely scenarios. Who is the least likely person to commit a murder? A baby (too far-fetched!)? An old lady? A policeman? A priest? Then starting asking *What if* questions.

Let's try another genre: *Westerns*. What can happen? Cattle rustling, innocent man jailed for murder, the need to clear a father's name, win back the stolen ranch... the list is almost endless, and so are the number of possible *What ifs*...

A trigger for the what if that works for me is reading the synopsis of a published bestseller. For example, this one for *Hawke: Showdown at Dead End Canyon* by Robert Vaughan (Hawke is the series character):

> There's no peace for Mason Hawke from the ghosts of his past. A drifter and a loner, he's not looking for trouble when he rides into Wyoming Territory — but it's waiting for him nonetheless. Coming to the rescue of a wealthy landowner's daughter who was kidnapped by a pair of inept outlaws, Hawke finds himself an unlikely hero in a town called Green River.
>
> But his unsought celebrity has earned him some powerful enemies, including a land-hungry lady with a crooked official in her pocket and a ruthless killer on a leash. It seems justice is an illusion in this place where fraud and fortune-hunting dance with cold-blooded murder. But all that is about to change in a brutal hail of gunfire now that Hawke has come to play.

This looks like a great story. Let's try the *What if?*

What if the landowner's daughter was accidentally killed in a gunfight, and the landowner blames the hero?

What if the character of the 'land-hungry lady' can be the landowner whose daughter died? Do you see the bones of a totally different story slowly building?

2. Write An Opening Line

The opening line of any novel or screenplay is often

crucial. Here's a trick that's been employed in many creative writing classes to get the creative juices flowing. We'll write an "opening line" or two that will probably never see the light of day but will hopefully generate story ideas.

Let's stick with the idea of a Western novel. How might it open?

When he rode over the brow of the hill, Hank Jenkin had no idea he was riding into a range war.

Or...

Big Jake shot the Marshall on Tuesday. By Thursday, the Mayor had run out of suitable candidates and had come to see me.

Or...

The saloon was unusually quiet for a Saturday night. It might have had something to do with the two dead bodies lying on the blood-splattered sawdust.

If you're anything like me, you'll change your sentences three or four times and then want to carry on writing until the idea is almost fully formed. That's fine.

Don't worry about grammar, characters, names, or spelling mistakes at this stage. You are only writing to generate an idea. Just keep going until you have a usable story.

3. Plundering The News

You read in a newspaper or online that :

- *An airliner containing 116 passengers has disappeared over the Sahara desert.*
- *A schoolboy returns home and finds his parents dead in their swimming pool.*
- *A previously unknown species of fish has been found in Antarctica.*

These are just three fairly typical stories from an average day's news. In this case, they were taken from a newspaper website on the day I'm writing this.

So what, you may be asking? None of these items is particularly earth-shattering. But let your imagination start to run wild and see where it takes you.

An airliner has gone missing. It'll probably turn up, but what if it doesn't? Has it been hijacked or blown up? Is it a robbery or a kidnapping? How do the bad guys prevent a captured plane from being tracked by the authorities? There are lots of questions that could provide the basis for a great adventure novel.

The son returns home and finds his parents' bodies floating in the swimming pool. The real story was that this was a tragic double accident but supposing they'd been shot? Or ritually murdered? Who might have done it? Was it a professional 'hit' or a crazed killer acting randomly? Again, this could offer a good start for a novel, especially if you play around with the facts.

Suppose the fish was carnivorous or maybe could communicate with its captors by telepathy. Maybe it's not a fish but a new species of intelligent ape? Perhaps the fish is the first to be found of a fast-breeding plague fish that might start eating people and maybe cause problems to the world's shipping routes.

Lots to think about there, right? And those are just three items from a single day's newspaper. Every day, every newspaper and news website in the world is crammed with ideas that could help you write your novel. Most of them might be even better than those exampled!

Why stop there? Go to a reference library and scan the specialist magazines and reference books. Google for strange phenomena. Spend a day digging deep in Wikipedia. Check out YouTube. I'm sure you'll soon be brimming over with great story ideas.

The Importance Of Outlining

All sensible authors work from some kind of outline. There are writers who'll tell you they prefer to *wing it* and make everything up as they go along. These guys are called 'pantsers' because they write by the "seat of their pants". You might choose to do this for future novels, but you should write from an outline for this one.

My method of writing a novel may seem a little 'top heavy', and I admit to spending many hours planning before I start putting down the words. The point is that all this forward planning really speeds up the total novel writing process. When I'm ready to write, I can let rip and watch the words pour out of me.

When they claim to be writing, most other authors are wasting time wondering about plot points, characters' motivations, and what colour Greyhound buses were in the 1940s.

I don't.

Because I spent a little more time in the planning stage, I can write thousands of words in a day without having to stop and ask, "What happens next?" The whole outlining process can take as little as a week, from idea to finished novel. If it takes any longer for you, don't beat yourself up about it. After all, practice makes perfect.

Without an outline, you are unlikely to finish your novel at all. I know from bitter experience how easy it is to get bogged down with silly plot points when you should be writing. The easy way to solve plot and story problems is at the outlining stage.

Trust me on this.

THREE

The Story

─────────────

WE ARE ALMOST ready to begin writing. But first, our journey needs a road map. If you're going to follow in the footsteps of the pulp fiction authors and write quickly with hardly any wasted words, you'll need to know in advance exactly what you're going to write.

This means having an outline.

How detailed an outline you end up with is up to you. Some authors prefer step-by-step guides that cover every scene in the novel. Others can get away with much less detail. It depends entirely on how you work.

Before we can start formulating a story, we need to know how stories are structured. This section briefly explains some of the most effective ways successful authors and screenwriters plot and structure their novels.

If you get confused, you'll find more information about story and plotting in my book, *How To Write The Million $ Dollar Story*. Please feel free to check it out.

These days, almost everyone uses the Three Act

structure. This is what is taught in schools and in most writing courses.

How the Three-Act Story Works

When you look at the biggest-selling books and movies, you'll see that their stories unfold in pretty much the same way. Many of Shakespeare's plays fit inside this template —though he was especially fond of 5- and 7-act structures.

At the beginning of any story, the characters are going about their normal lives, oblivious to the impending crisis that's about to rock their world. Then something big happens to disrupt the *status quo*. The protagonist (or protagonists) spends the rest of the story trying to solve the problem and get things back to normal. Welcome to the *Three-Act Structure*.

Almost any story can be divided into three parts or *Acts*: roughly conforming to the Beginning, Middle, and End. Act 2 is almost always the longest, usually, as long as Acts 1 and 3 combined.

Act 1 starts with characters living their normal lives. This establishes the scene and reveals who they are, and where they live. It's usual to hint at any potential weakness that will affect how the lead character(s) react later in the story. This could be a fear of heights, alcoholism, post-traumatic stress, or any one of a zillion other flaws.

Sometime during the first quarter of the book, often around the middle of Act 1, a major event will occur that will signal a radical change to the status quo. This is called the *Inciting Incident*.

This has to be something big: a *life-or-death moment*. In a Mystery novel, it might be a brutal murder the detective has to solve; in a Romance, it could be the moment Boy first meets Girl; in a Thriller, it might be when the hero's daughter is kidnapped.

Depending on the genre you are writing in, the *life and death struggle* doesn't have to be literal. For example, in a Romance or a Comedy, there probably won't be much physical danger. It can be a psychological challenge, or maybe a way of life that's under threat. The threat to flood a valley in order to build a dam, or chop down woodland, would count.

In the film, *Meet The Parents,* the inciting incident is the moment Pam receives the call from her sister announcing she's going to marry Kevin and Greg is forced to abort his own planned proposal. Then and there he realises that, in order to live the happy life he dreams of with Pam, he'll have to meet and impress her parents.

At this stage of a story, the protagonist is not usually fully committed to the Inciting Incident. The detective who has no emotional attachment to the murder case could always ask his boss to assign someone else. The lead in the Romance could decide not to get romantically involved. The kidnapped child's father could easily call in the police and leave it to them, and Greg could refuse to meet Pam's parents and start looking for another life partner.

If any of these characters reacted in this perfectly

normal way, there'd be no story. To save our novel we'll have to construct the *Act One Climax*, also known as the *Lock-In* or the **Point of No Return**. As you might expect, it occurs at the end of Act 1. Once it has taken effect, the protagonist is committed to taking action and cannot back down.

The Lock-In can be emotional, physical, or metaphorical, or it might be as literal as the lead character being locked in a cell or trapped in a cave. The detective might have a daughter the same age as the victim, or they might be about to be demoted and need to solve a major case to save their career. The father might be an ex-cop who messed up a case involving a kidnapped child and needs to redeem themselves, both professionally and in their personal life.

Maybe the protagonist in the Romance story considers themselves almost 'over the hill' — in other words, approaching old age — and views this as their last chance of finding a soulmate.

In the case of *Meet The Parents*, the Point of No Return is when Greg enters the Byrnes house and the door literally slams shut behind him. In *Gone With The Wind*, it's when news reaches Scarlett at the barbecue that the Civil War is about to be declared.

At the start of **Act 2**, the lead character has to be aware that the only way is forward. The detective will have to solve the murder, the kidnapped girl will have to be rescued, and so on. In *Meet The Parents*, in order to get what he wants (a happy life with Pam), Greg knows he has to win over her parents, especially her father.

Act 2 is where most of the action takes place. Your

protagonist will encounter major opposition and the reader has to believe he or she is vastly outnumbered and outgunned. To make people keep reading, you have to keep cranking up the action. Things have to get progressively worse, the protagonist has to suffer greater and greater reversals.

In the middle of Act 2 (the book's halfway point), comes the **Midpoint** or *First Culmination*. Not everyone uses this device, but I find it useful for splitting up the action in the double-length second act. It provides a natural break-off for the action in the first part of Act 2.

Sometimes the Midpoint will be positive for the protagonist, and at other times negative. Often the protagonist is allowed a brief partial victory, which is snatched away at the end of the act.

A good example of 'Midpoint reversal' can be found in *Meet The Parents*. Greg searches in vain for the Byrnes' cat, Mr Jinx, and eventually despairs and buys a looka-like from a pet rescue. At the Midpoint, he has become a hero, but at the climax of the act, he is denounced when the cat is found to be an impostor that has wrecked the house and ruined the wedding dress.

The Midpoint often signals a complete story rever-sal. In Alfred Hitchcock's classic *Vertigo*, the James Stewart character, Scottie, chases the woman he loves up the church tower, but he becomes paralysed by his fear of heights and cannot get more than partway up. He then watches in horror as Madeleine crashes to her apparent death.

Another way of using the Midpoint is to allow the protagonist to reflect on events that have occurred up to that point. They realise how far they've fallen from being the 'good' or 'successful' person they were in the opening chapters. They will either want to stop, or else it will act as a motivator to push them on against the hopeless odds. Or perhaps they are proud of what they have achieved and are spurred on by this realisation.

If the protagonist is driven to despair and wants to stop, you have to make them go on by providing some kind of outside stimulus. If it's a detective chasing a serial killer, you could factor in a particularly gruesome new murder or perhaps a specific threat to a family member or other loved one. If it's a fugitive on the run, send the cops crashing into the apartment, allowing him to escape by the skin of his teeth.

At the end of Act 2, comes the *Act Two Climax*, also known as *Plot Point II*. This is what pushes the story into Act Three, where everything is finally resolved. This Plot Point might be a line of dialogue, a victory in battle, or just the protagonist's realisation that everything has changed.

Sometimes it will be the opposite of what the audience has been expecting. Other times it's what we've been waiting for and dreading all along, like when the boat sinks in *Titanic*.

In *Meet The Parents* the climax to Act 2 is the realisation that Greg has been lying after the fake Mr Jinx wrecked the wedding dress. In *Thelma & Louise*, it's extremely subtle. The two women drive towards Mexico and reach Monument Valley. Louise stops the car to enjoy the night air and scenery. It suddenly dawns on her that it could well be her last night alive.

This silent realisation is the Act Two Climax. In the next scene, she shares her thoughts with Thelma and we move towards the movie's resolution.

Act 3 is where everything is settled. The final act is especially important because unless handled very carefully, it can undermine all your hard work in the previous two acts and leave your readers wondering, *Is that all?* That's a question all writers should dread.

Story Guru Robert McKee quotes a well-known Hollywood saying: 'Movies are about their last twenty minutes'. In the novel-writing world, you can say the same about the final few chapters.

Veteran detective writer Mickey Spillane summed it up when he declared: *The first chapter sells the book; the last chapter sells the next book.* This is particularly apt when you're writing for Kindle and relying on repeat sales.

The simplest way to achieve success in your final act is to ensure the ending is a climax rather than an anti-climax. You also have to make sure all loose ends are tied up. The ending has to be *plausible* though (if at all possible) *surprising*.

The ending is without a doubt the most difficult area to plot. There's so much to think about and so much to tie in, but I am afraid that your entire novel will be judged on how you handle it. That's probably why many successful storytellers start with the ending of the story and work their way back to the beginning.

It's becoming a requirement that certain types of stories feature a **Third Act Twist**, which sends events in a totally new direction. It's not a new phenomenon. In the classic movie, *Casablanca*, it's Rick putting Ilsa and Victor on the plane to Lisbon, while he stays behind with the corrupt Captain Renault. In Hitchcock's *Psycho*, the twist is the revelation that Norman's mother has been dead for years and that he's been impersonating her.

Get To Know Your Lead Characters

The lead characters are the most essential part of any story. Who they are and how they react is what your novel is all about. In its simplest form, every story is about a protagonist fighting an opponent.

In real life, the opposition may be a faceless corporation or simply The Mob, but that's not great for genre fiction. You'll get much more mileage out of the conflict if the opposition has a figurehead, someone the reader can recognise as the Bad Guy.

When you are writing a novel, even *pulp fiction*, it is essential that you know your characters intimately. Writing is so much easier if you instinctively know how they would react to any given situation. I discovered a quick and easy trick to get to know the people in my novels. I'll reveal it to you if you promise not to tell anyone.

First of all, you need to sort out all the stuff that only applies to your genre and to your story. From your own reading and research, you'll know roughly the kind of lead character your readers will most identify with. Having said that, it's important you make your protagonist as distinctive a character in his or her own right as you possibly can, especially if you are planning a series.

It's crucial you do not copy a character created by another writer. When I was an editor at a publishing house, I was amazed at how many new authors thought it was a great idea to write about a detective character in modern London who is Sherlock Holmes in all but name (and the author's writing ability).

When I'm creating new characters, my first move is to think of a film or TV star who'd be most suitable to play him or her when (!) they film the novel. I'm a bit of a classic movie buff and so I usually go for stars of the 1940s-1960s. Actors like Robert Mitchum, Kirk Douglas, Burt Lancaster, Jane Russell, Veronica Lake, and Alan Ladd, but that's just me.

It might help to go through lists of actors in movies on websites like Amazon and IMDb.

Having picked a suitable actor, I then search for an image showing them looking something like my character might – similar clothing, expression, hair, and so on. I now know roughly what my protagonist looks like. Because these stars are versatile actors, they'll be able to play the part of your character, so it won't just be a case of Tom Cruise playing Maverick in *Top Gun* playing your protagonist. It will be Tom Cruise playing the lead in your book. That's important to remember: you are *casting*, not *copying*.

Now you need to define characteristics. I have a list I use for all my characters. Thanks to the actor you chose, you'll already have some idea of the physical look, the rest can be worked out as you go along.

- **Character name:**
- Any nicknames (and why):
- Age:
- Height:
- Physical features:
- Usual style of dress:
- Personality:
- Politics:
- *Background: Including place of origin, manner of speech and vocabulary.*
- *Mannerisms: It pays to give each of your characters a little foible. Stroking the nose when stressed, tapping fingers as if listening to music (as my Dad used to) when watching sports, constantly eating mints, or whatever. Just don't overdo it when you come to write the novel. Occasionally, you might not even mention the mannerism at all.*

- *Back story: Father, mother, school (good scholar?) after school and everything up to the start of the novel.*
- Strengths & Weaknesses:
- What does this character want above everything else:
- What does this character most dread:
- Favourite food, movies, TV shows, songs and books (if appropriate):
- Drinking (& if applicable, drug) habits:
- Five things this character might say (apropos nothing):

- Some of this stuff will never be included in any of your novels, but it's helpful if you know a little more about your characters than the reader. I like to start with profiles of the protagonist, the lead bad guy and anyone else who might potentially play a major role in the story.

If you don't yet know the answer to any of these questions, it's perfectly OK to leave one or two of them for later.

How to Create An Outline

There's more than one way to skin a cat and more than one way to outline a novel. I've personally used several methods throughout my writing career and I've found most of them wanting in one way or another.

In previous editions of this book, I demonstrated a single method I used to use. It worked fine for a while, but I knew I could do better.

I deliberately went out to see if I could find a better way of outlining. I checked out a *Masterclass* with James Patterson, I read just about every book I could find on the subject. In the end, I realised I was on my own. I had to formulate a new system from what I'd seen and from what I knew. It took me literally weeks to work out. The good news is, it works like a dream.

This is a summary of how I outline…

It Starts with an Idea

If you followed the methods described in the last chapter, you should already have a basic idea for your novel. It's time to expand this germ into a fully-fledged story.

First, we need to add some basic details. If we don't already know where the story takes place, or when, it's something we need to decide on right away. It might be Paris in 1845 or present-day Chicago. It could even be Mars in the year 2525. The possibilities are almost endless but the setting will have a huge influence on how the story evolves. For example, they didn't have passenger jets in 1865 (so no 'Snakes on a Plane'), and a Romance set in 1942 Paris would have been under German Occupation. Unless you're deliberately writing historical fiction, the 'present day' is easiest.

Having decided on a setting and location, I like to work out the ending. With a Mystery story, I will have an idea of who is murdered and why. I will also have a detective in mind. So, how will the novel end? Will the detective catch the killer, if so (it's usually a good idea), will there be a twist in the tail?

When I've worked out the ending and the twist, I now have a beginning and an end. I also have a crime, a detective and (hopefully!) I know who did it. The next step is to fill in the gaps.

Remember: none of what you're doing is set in stone. You can always come back and change something if you get a better idea. In fact, that's the joy of this system. It's a great way of generating brilliant ideas.

I find it easier to work into the middle, which

means I go from thinking about how the story ends to working out how it started.

I ask myself, what was life like in the beginning, before all the drama started to unfold? The inciting incident will generally be pretty obvious (the central murder, boy meets girl, war is declared, and so on).

I then work my way through the various plot points, filling them in as best I can. Often, I will write down something vague, such as 'detective has a problem' or 'something bad happens to Laura' and come back to it later.

As a reminder, here is a simplified version of the Three Act structure:

ACT 1
Beginning (normal life)
Inciting Incident
Point of No Return

ACT 2
Conflict (1)
Midpoint
Conflict (2)
Act 2 Climax

ACT 3
Conclusion
Twist in the Tail (optional)

The Story Synopsis

Having worked out the elements of a basic story, I find it's a good idea to convert what you have (which may not be much at this stage) into several paragraphs of prose. I write informally as if I am telling a friend what happens. It doesn't need to be perfect or very detailed. At this stage, we will be constantly adding to and improving our story. Nothing is fixed.

I'll write something like this:

Detective Inspector Anna Chilcot of the Metropolitan Police Anti-Terrorism Unit is awoken by a call about a suicide bomber at Heathrow Airport. Anna works on intelligence-gathering, and it seems the bomber is the husband of one of her subjects. By the time she gets to the airport, the bomb has been detonated, and two police officers have been killed.

At the airport, Anna discovers that an undercover unit has been following the bomber and that the woman's husband has disappeared. Anna suspects that she is not being given all the information she needs. She is taken off the case when she presses her superiors and is assigned routine duties.

Whilst working on administration, Anna secretly continues to investigate the bombers and starts to suspect that a secret government agency was encouraging an attack for political purposes. A member of the secret agency stumbles upon Anna's snooping, and she is discredited and forced to go on the run.

The story ends with Anna exposing a group of politicians using the secret military agency (think of a name!) to engineer a coup against the government, which they consider 'too soft' on law and order. Anna is framed on espionage charges and ends the novel in prison.

As you write, you may find that ideas come to you seemingly out of nowhere. Don't be afraid to change direction when something better comes up.

Scenes & Chapters

The next step in the process is to convert the action into scenes. Unless you're writing a stream-of-consciousness novel, your story will consist of a series of events. This is where some people get confused.

A scene in a novel is not the same as a scene in a movie. Take the case of two detectives discussing a murder victim. They start in the Lieutenant's office, then walk down the corridor to the elevator. They travel down to the ground floor, and out through the lobby into the street, then stroll into the coffee shop. In a novel, that'd be one scene. In a movie, it'd be six.

In film, every change of location demands a new scene.

A chapter can consist of just one scene, or it can have several. Modern authors like James Paterson write thrillers with over a hundred chapters, most of them containing a single scene. The main advantage of doing this is that it's easy to generate pace.

When you break down your story into scenes and chapters, I suggest you look to the genre novels you examined during your Amazon research for guidance.

They'll show you what your readers expect and, even more importantly, what will work stylistically. When you're a writer, it's perfectly fine to let someone else do your hard work.

I used to use index cards, one for every scene. By arranging them in order – I used to do it on my dining room table – you can move the cards around and discard any that don't fit in. Usually, I'd find myself writing new scenes, which I discovered was the easiest way to get myself out of most story problems.

I say *used to use index cards* because several years ago, I came across writing software called Scrivener. That's what I'm writing with right now. I don't have any commercial interest in Scrivener. I just think it's a useful writing tool that's full of great features. What attracted me in the first place was the virtual corkboard with index cards for plotting purposes. You can try Scrivener for free for 30 days by going to www.litera tureandlatte.com/scrivener/download.

At this stage, I try to keep everything as simple as possible. The top line of my index card carries the scene's title, and below it I write a very brief synopsis of what happens. In Scrivener, it might look like this:

> ▭ **Police interview with Carl Bailey 1**
>
> At the police interview, DCI Connors notices that Carl does not flinch when he says he was at home when Taylor called, which the police know is untrue. Connors now knows that Carl is a very good liar. Throughout the interview Carl gives vague answers and eventually goes "no comment". Connors decides to look for...

Having got your scenes into some kind of order, the next stage is to create chapters. At the end of the process, you should have a list of scenes within chapters in the order you want to use them. Now comes the time to add the detail.

If you want the full story, check out my complete ebook, *Outline Your Books Or Die!*, available from Amazon as part of this collection.

Another Way To Outline

Successful British Thriller writer Ken Follett uses an interesting technique. He starts his outline by writing a single sentence. Then he turns the sentence into a paragraph and keeps expanding the story until he has produced a detailed synopsis or outline. Each enlargement makes him consider the story's specifics in easy-to-manage chunks.

He might begin with:

German spy in Wartime Britain has information vital to the result of the war and must be stopped from getting it back to

Berlin.

This is refined and added to. The next version might look like this:

In 1944, a ruthless German spy called Henry Fodel (known as die, Nadel, 'the Needle'' because of his use of the stiletto knife to kill) is the only known enemy agent at large in Britain. He discovers that the Allied Invasion will be aimed at Normandy (how?), and he makes his way to Scotland, where a German submarine is waiting for him.

Keep adding to it and elaborating, and you will soon end up with an outline for your novel. I found that having a rough idea of the overall story and then deciding on plot points at quite an early stage really helped me. The plot points I start out with are usually wildly different by the time I've finished writing the synopsis/ outline. Think of them as pins on a map that can be moved around to where they do the most good.

The Devil Is In The Detail

Most authors do their research right at the beginning of the novel-writing process before they have any real idea of their story. I find this incredibly wasteful.

By performing detailed research *after* I've completed my outline, I need only look for information I know I can use. Instead of it taking weeks or months, research can only take me a day or two. Sometimes I can do everything I need to in a couple of hours. It all depends on how well I know the subject before I begin.

The next stage involves going through the index cards (or whatever you are using) and filling in the gaps. I describe in reasonable detail what happens in each scene. There are two reasons for this. The first is that it makes the writing process easier if I don't keep having to stop and think things through. I like to do the thinking before I start writing.

I also find it easier to spot inconsistencies at this early stage. When I'm writing thousands and thousands of words, I can't always notice that Mike was Mack until chapter six.

Be as specific as you are going to be in the novel. Don't say, Jack goes from Smith's office to Covent Garden, where he meets Lisa, add as many details as you think you'll need: Jack took a black cab from Smith's office near Marble Arch to Covent Garden. It dropped him off in The Strand and he walked up Southampton Row until he came to the Piazza. Lisa met him outside the Apple Store and they went to Maggie's Coffee Shop in Floral Street for coffee. Although the geography is correct (Google Street View is useful for that), Maggie's Coffee Shop is a figment of my imagination.

Remember how we made biographies for our main characters a little while ago? I like to do this for everyone who appears in the novel. There's no need to go into as much detail, just enough to know who they are, how they'd react and how they'd speak.

FOUR

Writing

WE ARE NOW in the happy position where we can sit down and write the novel. Strictly speaking, the index cards and outline we've made can be counted as a first draft.

Well done!

A while ago, it was common for writers to be taught to knock out a first draft as quickly as possible and then discard it, moving on to the next. Stephen King suggests a version of this in his book, *On Writing*. He says it's a good way to get plot points reconciled and the author introduced to his characters and story. This is supposed to make the second draft so much better. Then the advice is to scrap the second draft and write a third. That's three whole novels. *What a monumental waste of time and creative energy!*

In the days of the Pulp Fiction authors, writing to live was so much more difficult than it is today. They had only manual typewriters to work on (if they were lucky), and editing effectively meant rewriting everything from scratch. This meant they tried very hard to get it right the first time.

You've got to try and do the same. When you sit down to write, it's important that you write, not gaze out of the window, pick your nose, or visit Facebook. Get as many words down 'on paper' as you possibly can. Don't forget, you then have the luxury of being able to edit everything afterwards on your computer.

Before You Sit Down

It's important you try and make time to write every working day. Most writers perform better if writing is part of a regular routine rather than something they pick up and drop every so often.

The time you pick to do your writing is up to you. Some writers (like me) prefer the morning, while others write best in the evening or in the dead of night. Try as many options as you can, and pretty soon, you'll find a routine that works for you.

Remove as many distractions as possible. Stuff like Facebook, Twitter, phones, and your email app should all be switched off. Your writing time cannot be shared with anyone or anything else.

Spouses, children and friends have to realise that you are totally unavailable during your writing time, except for the direst of emergencies. This is often the hardest part to get right. The easiest option is to write when they're not around. That's why so many writers take their laptops or tablets to a coffee shop or library and work there.

Writing a complete novel is far more daunting than simply writing a series of scenes or chapters. That's why we're going for the easiest option and writing in instalments. One chapter at a time.

Because you are going to write non-stop until the scene or chapter you are working on is finished, you need to know exactly what will happen. Some authors write a brief synopsis before they sit down to write each segment so that everything is fresh in their minds.

I type the segment synopsis on the page before I begin to write. It gives me something to refer back to if I get stuck. I call writing this chapter synopsis 'warming up' because it limbers me up for the writing I am about to do. I find it incredibly useful, and it lets me 'hit the ground running'.

Focus

Once you start writing, you have to focus 100% on the world you are creating for your novel. The human mind is notorious for thinking up other things that are 'more important' than writing. It will say things like: *You don't stand a chance of becoming a published novelist, so why are you wasting your time? Your work is so far below what's acceptable, it's embarrassing.*

When that doesn't work, it might attack from a different direction:

Surely, a cup of coffee would help you concentrate? Maybe rereading that passage about 'Focus' in Jim's book will give you more inspiration. Doesn't the cat need feeding? It would be cruel not to give Mr Jinx his morning snack…

Ignore everything your mind is telling you. Just write.

You have to let the words flow onto the page. Write as fast as you can. Don't stop to look over what you've just written. Just keep writing.

With me, it takes a few minutes for me to get into the flow of writing (that's why the 'warm up' is so useful). From speaking to others, this appears to be quite normal. I really have to force the first few paragraphs, but once the writing takes hold, the words start to flow and I feel exhilarated.

The important thing is to write as many words as your scene or chapter requires. No more, no less. When you get to the end, stop. Each chapter you write brings you closer to your eventual goal: a completed novel.

Sprinting

A technique that works for many people is to write like this (fast, without stopping) but in short, bursts called 'sprints' over a set period of time. Start with ten minutes. Write as much as you can in those ten minutes. When you're done, take a break. Make a coffee, go for a walk, and answer emails. Anything that's not writing your book.

Gradually increase the duration of your sprints by 5 minutes. Maybe stop when you get to 30 minutes. At this stage, anything over that seems less of a sprint and more of a slog. Pick a length that suits you. Some people like the 30-minute sprint, but most writers say they prefer 15-20 minutes. It's up to you.

When you get into the flow of writing like this, you may find that longer periods might suit you. I now feel most comfortable with an hour, but I can only manage to do one or two hours a day.

Some people edit after each sprint, while others wait until the end of the writing day. Because of the intensity this method of writing requires, I like to keep going until I feel satisfied I've done enough. Then I edit.

Don't be fooled; even three hours (with breaks) of concentrated writing bursts can produce a lot of words. When I started out using this method, I wrote up to 800 words every 20-minute sprint. Every day was a 2,000-word day. Now I'm more practised I'm disappointed if I don't produce 5,000 perfectly usable words of a novel in the course of a single day. I know writers who regularly churn out 10,000 words a day, almost all of which end up in print. Even Stephen King would be pleased with that.

If you want to know more about how I learned to write more quickly (and, believe me, if I can do it, anyone can!), feel free to check out my book, *1800 Words An Hour*, which delves much deeper. You can get it free by joining my email list click here.

Keep it Snappy!

You need to make your novel as readable as possible. Make your readers happy, and they'll come back for more. Every writer develops their own writing style over time. The best, and most successful, authors hone their writing down to something everyone can read easily and understand. I forget who said it, but I firmly believe that every writer should aim for that 'simple elegance'.

When writing genre fiction, I suggest you follow the example of the greats and keep things short and snappy. Short chapters, short paragraphs, short sentences. Doing that will instil momentum that will keep your readers eager to stay with you and your story.

Don't use a long word when there's one shorter and more commonly used that will serve the same purpose. Keep adverbs to a minimum (Elmore Leonard says to eliminate them altogether, which seems a little extreme to me), and don't make the reader have to stop reading to look something up.

Of course, you may want to vary the pace from time to time by using longer sentences and paragraphs to show time passing more slowly or to emphasise a particular point. Pacing is a major cannon in the writer's arsenal, and that's good. But I can't see any reason to drop in obscure words or phrases or to use long, involved clauses and sub-clauses. If the reader has to go back and read something again to understand what the hell's going on, the writer has failed.

Here's an example of simple, effective prose. It's the opening sequence from the first Doc Savage novel, *Man of Bronze*, written by Lester Dent (under the house 'writing name' of Kenneth Robeson) in 1933.

There was death afoot in the darkness.

It crept furtively along a steel girder. Hundreds of feet below yawned glass-and-brick-walled cracks — New York streets. Down there, late workers scurried homeward. Most of them carried umbrellas and did not glance upward.

Even had they looked, they probably would have noticed nothing. The night was black as a cave bat. Rain threshed down monotonously. The clammy sky was like an oppressive shroud wrapped around the tops of the tall buildings.

One skyscraper was under construction. It had been completed to the eightieth floor. Some offices were in use.

Above the eightieth floor, an ornamental observation tower jutted up a full hundred and fifty feet more. The metalwork of this was in place, but no masonry had been laid. Girders lifted a gigantic steel skeleton. The naked beams were a sinister forest.

It was in this forest that Death prowled.

Death was a man.

He seemed to have the adroitness of a cat at finding his way in the dark. Upward, he crept. The girders were slick with rain, treacherous. The man's progress was gruesome in its vile purpose.

That is simple yet elegant writing. The descriptions are concise but atmospheric. The pace can't help but push the reader along. I want to know what happens next. If ace-plotter Dan Brown wrote like this, the critics would declare him a genius.

No Padding

When writing a novel, it's tempting to add extra words or scenes that will help you finish earlier or make your writing 'fuller'. *Don't do it!*

Padding is one of the greatest sins an author can commit. You write these words, sentences, and paragraphs to hit a word count target. *Adding an adjective here, an extra line of unnecessary description there...* Most of us have done it, but it must be avoided.

Adding extra words slows down your writing speed and makes the finished product flabby and less attractive. Successful authors make every word count. There's no room in Pulp Fiction or in Kindle ebooks for padding.

You might think the Pulp writers had a great incentive to add extra words to their books. After all, they were paid by the word, so the more words they wrote, the more they'd get paid, right? *Wrong.*

Pulp writers were selling finished stories. Stories that made readers want to come back for more. To make a satisfactory living meant they had to write quickly and simply. The faster they finished, the faster they'd get paid and the more stories they could write.

Aside from anything else, if no one liked their books, the publishers would stop buying them.

Don't let word counts dictate your writing. They should only ever be used as guides to help you plan and write a novel. If you aim for 70,000 words and the finished book is only 66,550, it's not the end of the world. It'll do. The last thing you should do is go through and insert 3,450 extra words — unless the book needs it, of course.

Similarly, if you come in over what you had expected to write, and you're sure there's no extra flab to be cut away, don't sweat it. In the glorious world of self-publishing, you are the boss and what you say goes.

FIVE

After Writing

WHEN YOU'VE WRITTEN ALL your scenes and chapters, your novel is all but finished. All that's left is to tidy up and polish it before you send it to a proofreader and/or editor.

This is where you'll differ from pulp authors of the past. They didn't have a lot of time for editing their own work and, anyway, they were writing to a formula and had stringent deadlines. If you're a writer self-publishing online, you also take on the responsibilities of the publisher, which means making the copy as perfectly readable as you can. Readers will penalise you if you don't, they'll demand refunds, review accordingly, and stop buying your books.

Personally, I like to take a few days off from the characters before I start editing. I might try writing non-fiction or else devote my time to researching a new project. When you come to edit your novel it's important your head is as clear of preconceptions as possible.

Before you do anything, it's important you make a

new file. I usually stick a number after the novel title like this: 'War_and_Peace_02'. This is the file I'll be editing, leaving the original on another hard disk, pen drive, or up on the cloud for safety's sake. Maybe all three — I'm very cautious.

Self-Editing

Some authors print out the entire novel and work with pen on paper, the old-fashioned way. If you think that will work for you, do it. I prefer self-editing on screen.

Read it Out Loud

There's nothing like reading your novel aloud to spot typos and extra words you'd normally miss. Plus it's a great way to discover sections and sentences that don't make sense. If you can find somewhere to do this (the coffee shop isn't ideal), all well and good. Reading aloud will take longer, but I find it's worth the extra time.

I'll not try and correct typos and story problems in the same edit. Each of the two processes seems to require a different part of the brain; when I've tried in the past, the results have been disastrous.

This means two separate edits.

The first is when I read out loud, the second is usually much less demanding because most potential story problems will already have been ironed out in the outlining stage.

The Two-Pass Edit

I speak the novel through once, looking for typos, mistakes and sentences where the meaning isn't 100% clear. You can use your computer's spelling and grammar checker to get rid of obvious howlers, but I find mistakes like double words (the *the*) and wrongly used words (*draw* instead of *drawer*) are easier to spot when you're reading aloud.

I make changes to the edit file as I go along. While I'm at it, I have a pen and a pad handy to write down any problems with the story I might find. On the first run, I merely want to eliminate typos and get a sense of the story as a whole. That's why I make those notes. You'd be surprised how often you can solve inconsistencies when you have an overview of the story in your head after you've proofed it.

Ask yourself searching questions, such as *Do I really need that scene? Could those four chapters be replaced by a single one?* Stuff like that. Don't expect to change the entire story: if everything seems in order, don't make drastic changes for the sake of it. You are still a pulp writer, don't forget. Speed is one of your objectives.

After the Edits

Not many novice authors realise that proofreader, editor, and copy editor are three separate jobs. In the world of traditional publishing, senior editors are high up in the hierarchy. They have the power to hire and fire authors and they'll only be interested in the broader picture of an author's work. Their role in life is to find and nurture commercially successful books and so they tend to focus on the big picture: setting, genre, characters, plot, and so on.

The traditional role of the copy editor is to do what we've just done: eliminate mistakes. After the copy editor has cleaned up a manuscript and the editor improved and approved it, the novel will be typeset and then proofread to eliminate any mistakes before it is ready to be sent off to the printing house.

In our world of self-publishing, most authors take on the roles of editor and publisher (not to mention marketing and sales director) themselves. This leaves copy editing and proofreading. Because you have done your research, you have to trust that you have created, written, and edited a potentially saleable novel. That's the editor's role taken care of. That just leaves copy editor and proofreader.

In this day and age, the majority of editors who work with self-published authors will be prepared to cover both roles. Most will eliminate any typos that manage to escape the self-editing process (you'll be surprised how many do!) as part of the copy edit.

A good editor will go through your words and, for a price, will correct all errors and make sure the novel is fit to publish. This being the case, why don't I eliminate the self-editing process and just send a finished manuscript (actually a computer file) straight to an editor?

I don't, for two reasons. The first is that doing the two edits myself means I can get to know my story and my characters better. This is especially important with a series. This will make me a better author and an author who writes better books. On top of that, if I send the editor a 'clean' manuscript (one as empty of errors as possible), she's going to charge me a lot less than if I sent her a bundle of mistakes and typos!

Freelance copy editors and proofreaders charge by the hour and the less work they have to do the less you'll end up paying. It could also save you time in the long run as my method avoids the possibility of seemingly endless backwards and forwards correspondence. This can take up a lot of time and money. Personally, I'd rather avoid all those problems.

It goes without saying that you should be careful who you employ. An English speaker with some basic editing experience at the bare minimum.

Just because someone is well-educated does not make them an editor. Editing is a skill that can be picked up over time (hopefully at someone else's expense) but it is better when it is taught.

I've found that copy editors who've worked for magazines and newspapers tend to be the best. Because they are used to working to a deadline they don't waste time changing things for the sake of it. At the same time, their aim is to make sure the writing is clear and precise. A perfect combination.

Before I found the editor I currently use, I tried several I'd found online. Most were pretty good, but one was terrible. Ironically, the terrible one charged the most!

Check out author forums and ask for references.

The cost can be anything from a few hundred dollars to thousands. Although it pays to shop around, the ultimate goal is to produce a great book. If money is an issue, get a literate friend or family member to do it. Despite what I've just said, this will be better than not having an editor at all. Who knows? It may be the start of their new career.

Listen to the Editor

You are the author and probably the publisher as well, so you are in charge. That goes without saying. But I strongly advise you to accept whatever advice your editor gives you.

Unless they are incompetent (in which case, why did you employ them?), it is likely the editor will know more about writing and publishing than you do. There is no point in paying someone to help you and then rejecting that advice because your ego has been bruised. Take it on the chin and let them help you make a better book.

Free Online Editing Tools

Various apps now offer spelling and grammar checkers, but there are generally more efficient resources available online. Although all have free versions (or offer a free trial), in almost all cases, joining up to the paid version gives you more and better options.

I'm unusual in that I use both Grammarly and ProWritingAid. Neither of them is cheap but I think the expense is justified. I find Grammarly is better for social media and online stuff, whilst ProWritingAid is more efficient in tackling grammar issues, which is where I need the most help when I'm writing.

In no order of preference:

Grammarly.com

ProWritingAid.com

Whitesmoke.com

Formatting & Publishing

The obvious next step after your novel has been written is to make it available to prospective readers. In the old days, this meant sending it off to an agent or publisher and having to wait several weeks for the rejection letter to arrive. Then you'd have to repeat the progress several times until you either gave up or eventually found a publisher.

That may be a cynical version of the way things worked before the Kindle Revolution, but it's pretty accurate. When I ran an independent publishing house in the 1990s, we used to publish up to 50 titles a year. Despite that, we'd typically receive the same number or more submissions every single week.

Inevitably, hundreds of people were always going to be disappointed. It took me a long time to periodically go through the manuscripts we kept receiving, and writers would get angry with me. It was a terrible system!

Now, things are much easier. You still have the choice of getting published by a mainstream print publisher, or you can opt to publish yourself online. There is now a middle ground: firms that will publish your novels online and market them professionally in return for a cut of the take. In the field of Crime and Mystery, Joffe Books in the UK has had enormous success. There are others.

You'll probably have noticed from the way this book is written that I'm a huge fan of Kindle and other self-publishing platforms. It's the equivalent of the Punk Rock movement of the mid-1970s. Anyone with a guitar (or in this case, a computer) can become a star. *Power to the people!*

Of course, it's a little more complicated than that. You have to format your novel and market your books yourself, which are two huge subjects in themselves. If you head over to the KDP Select website, they'll give you enough information until I can write a couple of books to show you how I do it.

In the meantime, keep on writing.

That's most of the writing stuff out of the way.

The next chapter starts with a history of Pulp Fiction, before reproducing some helpful writing advice from heroes of the genre. I've added it to later editions because of requests from readers.

I hope you enjoy reading this as much as I did researching it.

SIX

The Golden Age of Pulp Fiction

BACK TO BASICS: Pulp fiction is a generic name for popular, low-priced paperbacks and magazines. Printed on cheap 'pulp' paper, they peaked in popularity between 1910 and the end of World War II. Pulps offered mass-market escapist entertainment, sold not through bookstores but on newsstand racks and in corner stores.

They were the successors to the dime novels, penny dreadfuls, and short-fiction magazines of the Victorian era. Most were illustrated novel-length heroic stories featuring characters such as Doc Savage, The Shadow, Sexton Blake, and The Phantom Detective.

The typical pulp magazine in the USA had 128 pages, was sized 7 inches by 10 inches, with ragged, untrimmed edges. By comparison, magazines printed on higher quality paper were called 'slicks'.

It's generally accepted that the first pulp was Frank Munsey's *Argosy Magazine*, relaunched in 1896. Within a couple of years, its circulation had shot up from a few thousand to half-a-million. In 1903, dime novel publishers Street & Smith leapt aboard the bandwagon with *The Popular Magazine*, and were quickly followed by many others.

By 1934, pulp writer Frank Gruber estimated there were "no less than 150 magazines" on the go in the United States alone. The best-selling genres were adventure, crime, detective, fantasy, horror, science fiction, romance, 'spicy' (softcore erotic), and westerns.

Argosy, Adventure, Blue Book and *Short Stories* were the most popular, sometimes referred to as 'the big four'. Other leading titles included *Amazing Stories, Black Mask, Dime Detective, Flying Aces, Horror Stories, Love Story Magazine, Marvel Tales, Oriental Stories, Planet Stories, Spicy Detective, Startling Stories, Thrilling Wonder Stories, Unknown World, Weird Tales,* and *Western Story Magazine*.

The best-known British pulps included *Pall Mall Magazine, The Novel Magazine, Cassell's Magazine, The Story-Teller, The Sovereign Magazine, Hutchinson's Adventure-Story,* and *Hutchinson's Mystery-Story*. A German fantasy magazine called *Der Orchideengarten* had a format similar to the American pulps, printed on pulp paper and heavily illustrated.

During World War II, the paper shortage impacted publishers on both sides of the Atlantic. In 1941, *Ellery*

Queen's Mystery Magazine switched to a smaller digest size. They were quickly followed by almost all the competition. In 1949, Street & Smith shut down practically all its pulp magazines to move upmarket and produce slicks.

The competition from television, comic books, and cheap paperback novels heralded the end of the pulps. Most commentators pinpoint the 1957 liquidation of the American News Company (the main distributor of pulp magazines) as the final straw that broke the camel's back. By then, many of the best-known titles, including *Black Mask*, *The Shadow*, *Doc Savage*, and *Weird Tales*, had already gone.

By the 1960s, mainstream publishers had taken over the pulp fiction market and had launched budget-priced paperback imprints that ran parallel with their usual output.

Crime and Mystery series characters were back in fashion, especially with a hardboiled edge. Stories featuring Micky Spillane's Mike Hammer and Earle Stanley Gardner's Perry Mason continued to entertain, and novels by Richard Prather's Shell Scott and John D MacDonald's Travis McGee were among the big sellers of the time.

During the last decades of the 20th century, mainstream publishers signed up a new generation of pulp authors and made them 'respectable'. Writers such as Elmore Leonard, Robert B Parker, Sara Paretsky, Charles Willeford, Val McDermid, George V Higgins, and James Ellroy, found themselves on the bestseller lists and lauded by critics.

Everything was going great for the multinational publishing houses: sales were up, everyone thought they were cool, their profits continued to soar, and there seemed to be no end in sight. Then, out of nowhere, the Internet arrived, and with it, Amazon and Kindle.

This brings us bang up to date...

How the Pulp Writers Wrote

In the preceding chapters, I have shown you how to harness the techniques of pulp fiction writers and use them to create fiction for the Digital Age.

The pulp writers of the past had to create their fiction with no better technology than a manual typewriter. You can bet your last lucky dollar that had Lester Dent, Edgar Wallace, or Dashiel Hammett been given access to a computer and/or Dragon Dictation software, they'd have given up their typewriters in a minute. We can only guess how prolific they could have been if they'd been armed with better equipment.

That being the case, with all our technological advantages, there's no excuse for us not to create just as quickly and competently as those pulp writers. We do have the disadvantage of modern-day distractions: the internet, email, social media, mobile phones, texts, etc., etc.

But we also have the off-switch.

So, what can the pulp writers teach us?

An anonymous author, writing in a 1946 edition of the *Writers Digest*, gave this advice to aspiring pulpsters:

"Get out of bed, make your coffee, do your business. Sit down at your typewriter and keep working until you've written enough to be proud of. Do this seven days a week, fifty-two weeks of the year, and you'll have earned the right to call yourself a writer."

He (or she) went on to give their Ten Commandments for a Successful Author:

1. Read as many published stories as you can and learn from them.
2. If you know the beginning, the middle and the ending of your story, and if it all makes sense, the rest should fall into place.

3. Don't pussy-foot around your story Get stuck into the action straight away. The reader doesn't want to wait.
4. Before you write a chapter, work out exactly what you're going to say in that chapter.
5. Anything that bores you will bore the reader and has to go.
6. Write every day for as long as you can. Anything less than ten usable pages is not acceptable.
7. Don't copy anything.
8. Make sure your dialogue advances the story. There's no room for idle saloon chatter.
9. Keep descriptions to a minimum and avoid cliches. Everyone knows night is black and rain is wet, you don't have to keep reminding them.
10. Keep it tight. Don't use any more words than you have to.

Despite the prejudice of some plodding writers, writing 'at the speed of sound' does not equate with writing badly.

Ray Bradbury wrote his classic *Fahrenheit 451* in just nine days on a rented typewriter. As he explained some years later:

"I had a newborn child at home, and the house was loud with her cries of exaltation at being alive. I had no money for an office, and while wandering around UCLA, I heard typing from the basement of Powell

Library. I went to investigate and found a room with 12 typewriters that could be rented for 10 cents a half hour. So, exhilarated, I got a bag of dimes and settled into the room, and in nine days, I'd spent $9.80 and wrote my story; in other words, it was a dime novel."

Everyone has to write in the way that suits them. One of my favourite pulp authors is Fredric Brown. After he'd died, his widow revealed how he hated to write and would do just about anything to avoid sitting at the typewriter. However, he knew he had to get stuck in, and he did. Brown's stories are some of the best ever written.

Brown often took a long bus journey when he was stuck at a plot point. *(I do the same — I knew I'd got it from somewhere!)*. Brown was a true innovator and something of a tortured soul. He once said:

"There are no rules. You can write a story, if you wish, with no conflict, no suspense, no beginning, middle or end. Of course, you have to be regarded as a genius to get away with it, and that's the hardest part – convincing everybody you're a genius!"

The point about this statement is that he's giving us the 'secret of writing' in reverse. He's telling us that a successful story needs:

- Conflict.
- Suspense.
- A beginning.

- A middle.
- An end.

It may sound obvious, but it's the simple stuff that counts. Although he didn't enjoy writing, Frederic Brown knuckled down and wrote, no matter how good or bad he felt. That's the only way a writer will be able to produce words. Excuses don't hack it, only words will do. Try and remember that.

On the other extreme to Fredric is Edgar Rice-Burroughs. He had an ego the size of a particularly obese African elephant and wrote vast amounts of prose. When still a salesman selling pencil-sharpeners, the future creator of Tarzan spent much of his time on the road, which meant he had plenty of time for reading. Ed didn't have much money to spare, so he tended to buy pulps. Later, he recalled:

> "…if people were paid for writing rot such as I read in some of those magazines, then I could write stories just as rotten. As a matter of fact, although I had never written a story, I knew absolutely that I could write stories just as entertaining and probably a whole lot more so than any I chanced to read in those magazines."

I'll finish this section with an interesting 'how-to-write' piece from one of the great pulp authors.

The Lester Dent Pulp Paper Master Fiction Plot

Lester Dent was an enormously successful pulp author whose 30-year writing career began in 1929. His greatest creation was heroic adventurer Doc Savage, who first appeared in the story 'The Man of Bronze' in March 1933. Dent wrote 165 of the 181 novel-length stories which appeared under the nom-de-plumes 'Kenneth Robinson' followed by 'Kenneth Robeson' (after another writer called Kenneth Robinson got in touch!).

Dent was being paid $750 a novel, an enormous sum in the era of the Great Depression. When the Doc Savage series came to an end in 1949, Dent continued as a successful writer of Mystery and Western stories under his own name. The last story that appeared in his lifetime was a Western called 'Savage Challenge', published in the February 22, 1958 issue of the *Saturday Evening Post*.

To accompany a 'how-to-plot' article published in the 1936 edition of *Writers Digest Yearbook*, Dent declared: "Most editors who say they don't want formula don't know what they're talking about."

I'm reproducing Dent's *Pulp Paper Master Fiction Plot* in full. To be totally honest, it has dated (well, it was written more than eighty years ago!) and only really applies to short pulp stories but even so, it does contain some brilliant advice.

Lester Dent's Pulp Paper Master Fiction Plot

This is a formula, a master plot, for any 6,000-word

pulp story. It has worked on adventure, detective, western and war-air. It tells exactly where to put everything. It shows definitely just what must happen in each successive thousand words.

No yarn of mine written to the formula has yet failed to sell.

The business of building stories seems not much different from the business of building anything else.

Here's how it starts:

A Different Murder Method For Villain To Use

A Different Thing For Villain To Be Seeking

A Different Locale

A Menace Which Is To Hang Like A Cloud Over Hero

One of these *Different* things would be nice, two better, three swell. It may help if they are fully in mind before tackling the rest.

A different murder method could be — different. Thinking of shooting, knifing, hydrocyanic, garrotting, poison needles, scorpions, a few others, and writing them on paper gets them where they may suggest something. Scorpions and their poison bite? Maybe mosquitos or flies treated with deadly germs?

If the victims are killed by ordinary methods, but found under strange and identical circumstances each time, it might serve, the reader of course not knowing until the end, that the method of murder is ordinary.

Scribes who have their villain's victims found with butterflies, spiders or bats stamped on them could conceivably be flirting with this gag.

Probably it won't do a lot of good to be too odd, fanciful or grotesque with murder methods.

The different thing for the villain to be after might be something other than jewels, the stolen bank loot, the pearls, or some other old ones.

Here, again one might get too bizarre.

Unique locale? Easy. Selecting one that fits in with the murder method and the treasure–thing that villain wants–makes it simpler, and it's also nice to use a familiar one, a place where you've lived or worked. So many pulpateers don't. It sometimes saves embarrassment to know nearly as much about the locale as the editor, or enough to fool him.

Here's a nifty much used in faking local colour. For a story laid in Egypt, say, author finds a book titled *Conversational Egyptian Easily Learned*, or something like that. He wants a character to ask in Egyptian, "What's the matter?" He looks in the book and finds, *"El khabar, eyh?"* To keep the reader from getting dizzy, it's perhaps wise to make it clear in some fashion, just what that means. Occasionally the text will tell this, or someone can repeat it in English. But it's a doubtful move to stop and tell the reader in so many words the English translation.

The writer learns they have palm trees in Egypt. He looks in the book, finds the Egyptian for palm trees, and uses that. This kids editors and readers into thinking he knows something about Egypt.

Here's the second instalment of the master plot.

Divide the 6,000 word yarn into four 1,500 word parts. In each 1,500 word part, put the following:

FIRST 1,500 WORDS

- First line, or as near thereto as possible, introduce the hero and swat him with a fistful of trouble. Hint at a mystery, a menace or a problem to be solved–something the hero has to cope with.
- The hero pitches in to cope with his fistful of trouble. (He tries to fathom the mystery, defeat the menace, or solve the problem.)
- Introduce *all* the other characters as soon as possible. Bring them on in action.
- Hero's endeavours land him in an actual physical conflict near the end of the first 1500 words.
- Near the end of first 1,500 words, there is a complete surprise twist in the plot development.

So far: Does it have *Suspense*?

Is there a *Menace* to the hero?

Does everything happen logically?

At this point, it might help to recall that action should do something besides advance the hero over the scenery. Suppose the hero has learned the dastards of villains have seized somebody named Eloise, who can explain the secret of what is behind all these sinister events. The hero corners villains, they fight, and villains get away. Not so hot.

Hero should accomplish something with his tearing around, if only to rescue Eloise, and surprise! Eloise is a ring-tailed monkey. The hero counts the rings on Eloise's tail, if nothing better comes to mind.

They're not real. The rings are painted there. Why?

SECOND 1,500 WORDS

- Shovel more grief onto the hero.
- Hero, being heroic, struggles, and his struggles lead up to:
- Another physical conflict.
- A surprising plot twist to end the 1,500 words.

Now: Does second part have *suspense?*
Does the *menace* grow like a black cloud?
Is the hero getting it in the neck?
Is the second part logical?
Don't Tell: Show how the thing looked. This is one of the secrets of writing; never tell the reader, show him. (He trembles, roving eyes, slackened jaw, and such.) *Make the reader see him.*

When writing, it helps to get at least one minor surprise to the printed page. It is reasonable to to expect these minor surprises to sort of inveigle the reader into keeping on. They need not be such profound efforts. One method of accomplishing one now and then is to be gently misleading. Hero is examining the murder room. The door behind him begins slowly to open. He does not see it. He conducts his examination blissfully. Door eases open, wider and wider, until — surprise! The glass pane falls out of the big window across the room. It must have fallen slowly, and air blowing into the room caused the door to open.

Then what the heck made the pane fall so slowly? More mystery.

Characterising a story actor consists of giving him some things which make him stick in the reader's mind. *Tag him.*

Build your plots so that action can be continuous.

THIRD 1,500 WORDS

- Shovel the grief onto the hero.
- Hero makes some headway, and corners the villain or somebody in:
- A physical conflict.
- A surprising plot twist, in which the hero preferably gets it in the neck bad, to end the 1,500 words.

Does: It still have *suspense?*

The *menace* getting blacker?

The hero finds himself in a hell of a fix?

It all happens logically?

These outlines or master formulas are only something to make you certain of inserting some physical conflict, and some genuine plot twists, with a little suspense and menace thrown in. Without them, there is no pulp story.

These physical conflicts in each part might be *different*, too. If one fight is with fists, that can take care of the pugilism until next the next yarn. Same for poison gas and swords. There may, naturally, be exceptions. A hero with a peculiar punch, or a quick draw, might use it more than once.

The idea is to avoid monotony.

Action:

Vivid, swift, no words wasted. Create suspense, make the reader see and feel the action.

Atmosphere:

Hear, smell, see, feel and taste.

Description:

Trees, wind, scenery and water.

The secret of all writing is to make every word count.

FOURTH 1,500 WORDS

- Shovel the difficulties more thickly upon the hero.
- Get the hero almost buried in his troubles. (Figuratively, the villain has him prisoner and has him framed for a murder rap; the girl is presumably dead, everything is lost, and the DIFFERENT murder method is about to dispose of the suffering protagonist.)
- The hero extricates himself using *his own skill,* training or brawn.
- The mysteries remaining–one big one held over to this point will help grip interest–are cleared up in course of final conflict as hero takes the situation in hand.
- Final twist, a big surprise, (This can be the villain turning out to be the unexpected person, having the "Treasure" be a dud, etc.)

- The snapper, the punch line to end it.

Has: The *suspense* held out to the last line?

The *menace* held out to the last?

Everything been explained?

It all happen logically?

Is the punchline enough to leave the reader with that *warm feeling*?

Did God kill the villain? Or the hero?

And that's all you need to know. Try your own. Let me know how it goes.

The Writers' VIP Club

SIGN up for my email list to receive free emails containing up-to-date writing tips and important news for writers. Click here to join Jim Driver's Writers' VIP Club and get your next book for free!

Please review this book!

THANKS FOR STAYING with me to the end. I hope you found the journey useful.

I'd really appreciate it if you could find the time to write a short review, whether good or bad. It helps me and it helps other readers.

Click here to leave a review on Amazon

Thank you!

About the Author

Jim Driver was born in Yorkshire, in the north of England, in 1954. After being kicked out of college for not studying law properly, he became a music promoter and festival organiser, before finally settling down as a writer, editor, and publisher.

Jim wrote about music, beer and food for *Time Out* magazine in London for almost 20 years and founded the acclaimed independent publishing house, The Do-Not Press, in the heady 1990s. He has ghost-written several novels and published even more under various names.

Jim now lives beside the seaside in Ramsgate, East Kent, and is currently working on a series of mystery novels.